Keto Diet Recipes

The Ultimate Cookbook With

Easy and Tasty Recipes

Ava Leyla

KETO DIET COOKBOOK

Contents

can be in any fashion deemed liable for any hardship or damages that may befall them after undertaking information described herein.

Additionally, the information in the following pages is intended only for informational purposes and should thus be thought of as universal. As befitting its nature, it is presented without assurance regarding its prolonged validity or interim quality. Trademarks that are mentioned are done without written consent and can in no way be considered an endorsement from the trademark holder.

WHATO WE KNOW BY KETOGENIC DIET?

The ketogenic diet is an **eating pattern. A very high fat intake, a moderate protein intake, and a very low carbohydrate intake** (between 20 - 50 g / day) induce a metabolic process called "**ketosis**". On the contrary, the detox diet, which prioritizes and helps to increase the consumption of fruits and vegetables, and which also favours the practice of intermittent fasting.

Initially, the ketogenic or keto diet was developed for those patients with pediatric epilepsy, although today, it has become famous for its role in weight loss. Although the best known is the standard ketogenic diet (SKD), there are different types of the ketogenic diet, which supposes an approximate distribution of **55-60% of fats, 30-35% of protein and only 5-10% of carbohydrates newspapers**.

WHAT DO WE UNDERSTAND BY KETOSIS?

Before explaining the concept of ketosis, we must first understand how glucose and fat metabolism works in our body.

Carbohydrates are the main source our body uses for energy production. When our body is deprived of carbohydrates (consumption between 20-50 g / day), as happens with the practice of the ketogenic diet, insulin secretion is drastically reduced, and the body enters a catabolic state, which forces the body to undergo certain metabolic changes and the process of **ketogenesis** kicks in.

The ketogenesis process kicks in to provide an alternative source of energy to glucose in the form of so-called **ketone bodies**. Therefore, **during the ketogenic diet, ketone bodies replace glucose as the primary source of energy in our body, which is known as ketosis.**

As long as the body is deprived of carbohydrates, our metabolism will remain in **the ketone state**.

BENEFITS OF THE KETO DIET

Many have been the benefits that have been observed during the practice of the keto diet, including:

- **Weight loss**

- **Reduction of hyperinsulinemia**

- **Improved insulin sensitivity**

- **Excessive fat loss**

DANGERS OF THE KETO DIET

Although it has gained a lot of fame lately, this diet is not without dangers and/or contraindications and **should not be done lightly and without professional supervision**. The best and safest way to go on a keto diet is to supervise a dietitian-nutritionist and your regular doctor.

Regarding contraindications, this diet is contraindicated in people with:

- **Liver failure**

- **Pancreatitis**

- **Innate fat metabolism disorders**

- **Primary carnitine deficiency**

- **Carnitine palmitoyl transferase deficiency**

- **People with diabetes on insulin / hypoglycemic agents**

So you must consult your doctor before starting this diet.

In terms of **side effects, in the short term**, people who start practicing a keto diet suffer from:

- **Fatigue**

- **Headaches**

- **Dizziness**

- **Sickness**

- **Vomiting**

- **Constipation**

- **Low tolerance for sport**

These symptoms are known as **"keto flu" or "keto flu"**. Although very annoying, they usually disappear after a few days or weeks when the body has adapted to the low-carbohydrate ketogenic state.

In contrast, **in the long term**, the following side effects have been described:

- **Hepatic steatosis (or "fatty liver")**

- **Kidney stones**

- **Hypoproteinemia**

- **Vitamin deficiency**

Therefore, while the benefits of following a keto diet have been widely reported, long-term adherence to it is a limiting factor. On the other hand, the sustainability of this diet has been questioned, and the prognosis of the effects of the diet after its discontinuation should be examined.

RECIPES

FILLED DUMPLINGS WITH SALMON & SPINACH

INGREDIENT

- ➢ 1 baking mix "Das Helle"
- ➢ 500ml water
- ➢ 40g apple cider vinegar
- ➢ For the filling
- ➢ 400g fresh salmon
- ➢ 300g leaf spinach
- ➢ 1 onion
- ➢ Coconut oil for frying
- ➢ Salt pepper

PREPARATION

Preheat the oven to 160 ° C with a fan oven.

Peel the onion and cut it into small cubes. Wash the spinach well

Heat coconut oil in the pan and fry the onion cubes for 2 minutes.

Add the spinach, collapse a little and season everything with salt and pepper.

In the meantime, prepare the baking mixture according to the instructions with water and apple cider vinegar.

Divide the dough into 2 equal portions and roll them into an oblong square with a rolling pin. It's best to place the dough between two layers of parchment paper so that it doesn't stick to your fingers and the table.

Cover half of the dough with the spinach filling and salmon and place the other half over the topping.

Press the edge together firmly. If you like, you can brush the surface with whisked egg yolk and cut into a diamond shape.

Bake the dumplings for 60 - 65 minutes at 160 ° C convection (with top and bottom heat, the baking time is extended by 5 - 10 minutes).

KETO COCONUT CAKES WITH CHOCOLATE FILLING

INGREDIENT

- ➢ 4 eggs
- ➢ 80g erythritol
- ➢ 1 teaspoon Baking powder
- ➢ 60g butter
- ➢ 40g coconut flour (available here)
- ➢ 4 teaspoons of Simply Keto Choco-Coco Cream

PREPARATION

Freeze the Choco-Coco Creme spoon by spoon in ice cube molds.

Melt the butter.

Add all the remaining ingredients to the butter and mix everything together well.

Pour half of the batter into ovenproof molds and press the frozen chocolate cream into the center.

Spread the rest of the dough on top and bake the cakes for 25 minutes at 175 degrees.

KETO CHOCOLATE STOLLEN WITH SPRINKLES

INGREDIENT

- ➢ 4 eggs
- ➢ 250 g quark (40% fat)
- ➢ 150 g powder erythritol
- ➢ 250 g almond flour
- ➢ 20 g gold flax flour
- ➢ 50 g coconut flour
- ➢ 200 ml warm, unsweetened almond milk
- ➢ 1/2 cube of fresh yeast
- ➢ 1 teaspoon sugar
- ➢ 50 g butter

- ➢ 100 g nut nougat cream
- ➢ 100 g ground almonds
- ➢ 80 g erythritol
- ➢ 80 g butter
- ➢ 1 pinch of sal

PREPARATION

Crumble the yeast in lukewarm almond milk, add 1 teaspoon of sugar and let the mixture rest for about 10 minutes.

Mix the remaining ingredients in a large bowl and then knead with the yeast mixture to form a smooth dough and let rise again for 30 minutes.

Roll out the dough into a rectangle on a floured (almond) work surface.

Melt the butter and mix with the nut nougat cream.

Spread the mixture on the dough and roll it up from the long side, divide in the middle and cut the two strands up to half lengthways. Wrap them around each other and press each end firmly.

Put the whole thing in a square loaf pan and bake in the oven for 25 to 30 minutes at 175 ° C top / bottom heat.

Melt the butter.

Mix the melted butter with the remaining ingredients for the crumble and knead well.

Sprinkle the crumble mixture in the form of small pieces on the hot cake.

Bake the chocolate Striezel with the crumble again for 15 minutes until the crumble is golden brown.

VEGETARIAN KETO CHEESE-NUT ROAST

INGREDIENT

- ➢ 200 g nut mix (walnuts, almonds, hazelnuts)
- ➢ 100 g seeds and seeds (pumpkin seeds, sunflower seeds, sesame oil)
- ➢ 200 g tomatoes
- ➢ 1 zucchini
- ➢ 2 large onions
- ➢ 150 g mountain cheese
- ➢ 3 eggs
- ➢ 20 g gold flax flour
- ➢ 1/2 bunch of dill
- ➢ 1 tbsp olive oil
- ➢ Salt, pepper, nutmeg to taste

PREPARATION

Roast the nuts and kernels in a large pan without adding any fat for 5 minutes.

Then let cool a little and then finely chop.

Peel and finely dice the onion.

Heat the large pan again and add 1 tablespoon of butter. Fry the zucchini grated and onion cubes for about 3 minutes.

Halve and core the tomatoes and cut the flesh into small pieces. Chop the dill.

Coarsely grate the zucchini and mountain cheese. Put the tomato pieces, zucchini and grated cheese in a large mixing bowl.

Now add the remaining ingredients and the zucchini-onion mix to the bowl and season.

Grease a square loaf pan and add the cheese and nut mixture. Smooth the surface and brush with 1 tablespoon of olive oil.

Bake the cheese and nut roast at 180 ° C top / bottom heat (160 ° C convection) for approx. 1 hour.

KETO LÁNGOS

INGREDIENT

- ➢ 50 g bamboo flour
- ➢ 20 g coconut flour
- ➢ 30 g gold flax flour
- ➢ 30 g psyllium husk powder
- ➢ 3 eggs
- ➢ 120 g quark (40% fat)
- ➢ 150 ml of lukewarm water
- ➢ 1/2 packet of dry yeast
- ➢ 1/2 teaspoon sugar for the yeast
- ➢ Grated cheese, garlic sour cream, fresh herbs
- ➢ Oil for deep-frying

PREPARATION

Pour the yeast into the lukewarm water, add 1/2 teaspoon sugar and let the mixture rest for about 10 minutes.

Mix the eggs and quark in a large mixing bowl.

Add all remaining ingredients and mix everything into a homogeneous dough.

Cover and let the dough rise in a warm place for about 60 minutes.

After letting the dough rise, knead it again and divide it into approx. 8 portions.

Roll out the balls about 1 cm thick into round cakes.

Put enough oil in a wide saucepan so that the flatbreads have enough space to swim in.

Heat the oil to 160 ° C and fry the Lángos for 2 - 3 minutes on each side.

Then drain on kitchen paper and serve with garlic sour cream and grated cheese.

KETO SALMON SPINACH ROLL

INGREDIENT

- ➤ 500 g fresh spinach

- ➤ 1 small onion

- ➤ 4 eggs

- ➤ 150 g smoked salmon

- ➤ 200 g cream cheese

- ➤ 1/2 teaspoon scrambled eggs deluxe spice mix

- ➤ Salt pepper

- ➤ Juice of 1/2 lemon

PREPARATION

Preheat the oven to 180 ° C top / bottom heat.

Either let the spinach thaw or, if the spinach is fresh, wash it and chop it into small pieces.

Peel the onion and cut into small cubes.

Sauté the onion cubes in a large pan for 2-3 minutes until translucent.

Add the chopped spinach and cook for about 10 minutes until the spinach has lost its water.

Put the eggs in a bowl and stir until frothy, then season with salt and pepper.

Then add the chopped spinach to the eggs and mix thoroughly.

Cover a baking sheet with parchment paper and grease it.

Spread the spinach and egg mixture on top and bake for about 25 minutes.

Then place the mixture on a damp tea towel, peel off the baking paper and roll it up. Let it cool down like this.

Season the cream cheese with salt & pepper.

Spread 3/4 of the cream cheese on the rolled-out dough.

Cover with slices of salmon and drizzle with lemon juice.

Roll the whole thing up again and tighten (either with the kitchen towel or cling film).

Finally, coat the roll with the rest of the cream.

KETO ALMOND BUTTER FAT BOMBS

INGREDIENT

- ➢ 60g coconut oil

- ➢ 40g organic almond cream with whey protein

- ➢ 1 pinch of salt

- ➢ 5 drops of vanilla flavor

- ➢ 20g powder erythritol

PREPARATION

If the coconut oil is too firm, warm it up.

Put all the ingredients in a bowl and mix them together.

Pour the liquid mass into a suitable silicone mold and place it in the refrigerator or freezer until the mixture has set.

KETO CURD BALLS

INGREDIENT

- ➢ 25g bamboo flour

- ➢ 10g coconut flour

- ➢ 15g gold flax flour

- ➢ 15g psyllium husk powder

- ➢ 2 eggs

- ➢ 50g quark (40% fat)

- ➢ 25g erythritol

- ➢ 75ml lukewarm water

- ➢ 1/4 packet of dry yeast

- ➢ 1/4 teaspoon sugar for the yeast

- ➢ Oil for deep-frying

- ➢ Erythritol for wallowing

PREPARATION

Pour the yeast into the lukewarm water, add 1/4 teaspoon sugar and let the mixture rest for about 10 minutes.

Mix the eggs and quark in a large mixing bowl.

Add all remaining ingredients and mix everything into a homogeneous dough.

Cover and let the dough rise in a warm place for about 60 minutes.

After the dough has proofed, knead it again.

In the meantime, heat the oil (the balls should be able to swim in it) in a small saucepan to 160 ° C.

Shape walnut-sized balls with your hands and deep-fry for a few minutes until golden brown (turning on all sides).

Then drain briefly in a sieve and then roll in erythritol.

SALMON ON KETO CRACKERS

INGREDIENT

- ➢ 1 tbsp ground almonds

- ➢ 100 g grated parmesan

- ➢ 10 g sesame flour

- ➢ 1 egg

- ➢ 1 pinch of salt

- ➢ 1 tbsp Lebensbaum garden herbs

- ➢ 100 g smoked salmon

- ➢ 100 g cream cheese

PREPARATION

Mix all the ingredients together.

Place 10 small heaps on a baking sheet lined with baking paper.

Bake the cheese crackers at 200 ° C for about 15 minutes.

Connect the crackers and let them cool down.

Season the cream cheese with salt & pepper and spread on the crackers.

Chop the salmon and place on top of the crackers.

EASY KETO POPPY SEED CAKE

INGREDIENT

- ➢ 1 pack of keto cake mix

- ➢ 400ml coconut milk

- ➢ 30g poppy seeds

- ➢ Zest of 1 lemon

- ➢ For the frosting

- ➢ 130 - 150g powder erythritol

- ➢ Juice of 1/2 lemon

PREPARATION

Rub the zest of the lemon and squeeze out the juice.

Thoroughly mix the cake mix with the coconut milk, poppy seeds and lemon zest.

Fill the dough into a square loaf pan.

Bake the poppy seed cake at 175 ° C fan oven for about 40 minutes.

Mix the powdered erythritol and lemon juice to a smooth glaze.

Take the cake out of the oven, let it cool down briefly and brush it with the lemon icing.

KETO BOOSTER HAZELNUT-CHOCOLATE FUDGE

INGREDIENT

- ➢ 90 g coconut oil
- ➢ 10g MCT oil
- ➢ 15g powder erythritol
- ➢ 10 g baking cocoa
- ➢ A few drops of nut nougat flavor
- ➢ 1 pinch of salt
- ➢ 1 tbsp chopped hazelnuts as decoration

PREPARATION

Line the baking dish with parchment paper.

Put the coconut oil, MCT oil and powdered erythritol in a mixing bowl and mix everything together.

Now add the remaining ingredients and mix everything into a homogeneous mass.

Now spread the fudge in the baking dish and smooth the surface.

Let the fudge harden in the refrigerator for 45 to 50 minutes.

Decorate it with chopped hazelnuts if you like and cut it into square pieces.

Keep the hazelnut chocolate fudge in the refrigerator so it doesn't get too soft.

KETO PETIT FOURS

INGREDIENT

- ➤ 1 pack of keto cake mix
- ➤ 400ml water
- ➤ 40 g coconut oil
- ➤ 50 g almond flour
- ➤ 60 g powder erythritol
- ➤ 90 g ground almonds
- ➤ 20 g of water
- ➤ 5 drops of bitter almond flavor
- ➤ 100g sugar-free white chocolate
- ➤ 125 g strawberry fruit spread
- ➤ 25 g sugar-free dark chocolate to decorate

PREPARATION

Put the keto cake mix in a mixing bowl, mix with water and knead into a homogeneous dough.

Spread the dough on a baking sheet lined with baking paper about 1 cm high and bake on the middle rack for about 20 minutes.

Then let the cake base cool down, turn it out and peel off the baking paper.

Cut the bottom into 3 equal rectangles.

Brush the strips with jam and place on top of each other.

Melt the coconut oil carefully.

Add all ingredients and knead to a uniform mass.

Roll out the marzipan on a surface dusted with powdered erythritol to the size of the top plate.

Place the marzipan plate on the top cake base and press down.

Then cut everything into small cubes.

Melt the white chocolate carefully.

Cover the cubes with the melted chocolate, carefully place on a wire rack and allow to dry.

Decorate the petit fours with sugar-free dark chocolate if you like.

KETO FLAN

INGREDIENT

- ➢ 40 g erythritol gold
- ➢ 15 g of water
- ➢ 20 g butter
- ➢ 120 g whipped cream
- ➢ 2 eggs
- ➢ 2 egg yolks
- ➢ 30 g erythritol

PREPARATION

Preheat the oven to 150 ° C fan oven.

Grease the casserole dishes with butter and set aside.

Put the erythritol gold, water and butter in a saucepan over medium heat and heat, stirring, until the sauce turns golden brown.

Spread the sauce evenly between the baking dishes and set aside.

In a mixing bowl, stir the remaining ingredients until smooth.

Pour the mixture into the casserole dishes.

Place the casserole dishes in a large dish and fill it with boiling water until it reaches about half the sides of the casserole dishes.

Bake the flan for 50 minutes to 60 minutes, until the edges are firm.

Then take it out of the oven and let it rest for another 10 minutes.

Let the flan molds cool in the refrigerator until ready to serve (about 1 hour).

To serve, remove the flan from the mold with a knife and place on a plate.

VEGAN KETO TART WITH CHOCOLATE GANACHE

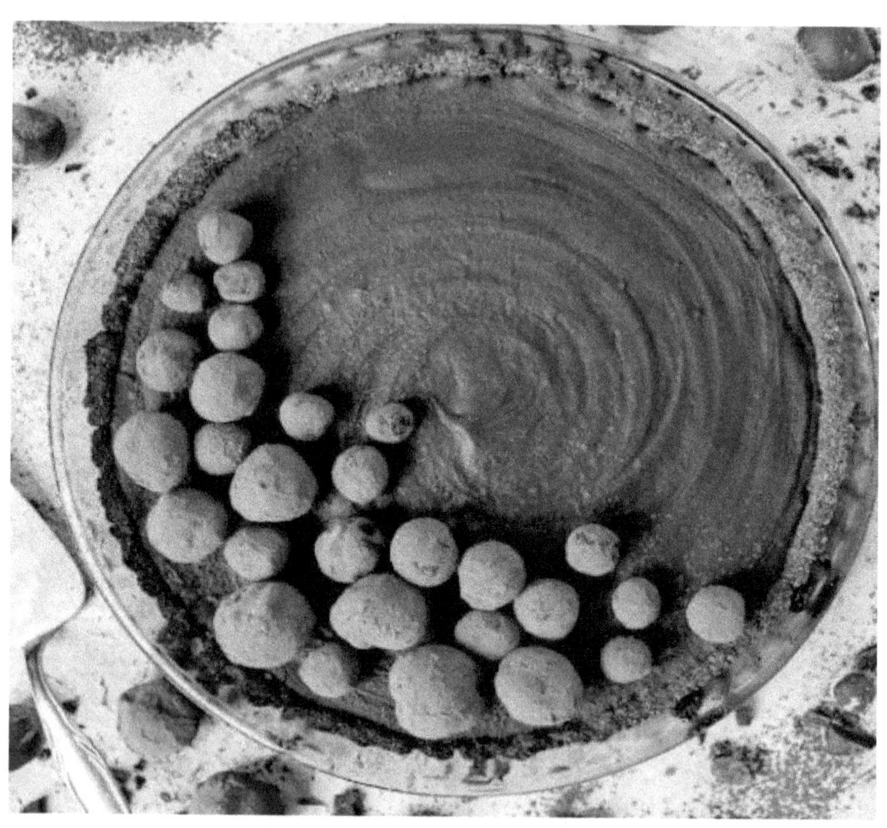

INGREDIENT

- ➤ 40 g almond flour
- ➤ 10 g gold flax flour
- ➤ 25 g ground almonds
- ➤ 20 g coconut flour
- ➤ 10 g baking cocoa
- ➤ 40 g erythritol

- ➢ 30 g coconut oil
- ➢ 225 g Simply Keto Dark Chocolate Drops
- ➢ 200 ml coconut milk
- ➢ 20 g coconut oil
- ➢ 18 cm cake pan

PREPARATION

First, melt the coconut oil.

Put all the ingredients for the base in a mixing bowl and stir them together until a sticky batter is formed.

Spread the dough over the entire bottom of a baking pan and form a rim about 1 cm high. TIP: We recommend a silicone baking pan. If you don't have one, line your shape with parchment paper.

Bake the cake base for about 15 - 20 minutes at 175 ° C fan oven.

Heat coconut milk and coconut oil in a small saucepan until almost boiling.

Add the chocolate drops and let them melt.

Mix everything together well and distribute evenly on the cake base.

Decorate with vegan truffles if you like.

LOW-CARB KETO BOOSTER CARAMEL AND ALMOND SHAKE

INGREDIENT

- ➤ 200ml almond milk
- ➤ 2 tbsp Simply Keto Creamer
- ➤ 15 drops of caramel flavor (available here)
- ➤ 2 - 3 ice cubes
- ➤ 1 tbsp erythritol stevia powder
- ➤ 1 tbsp almond butter (available here)
- ➤ Erythritol Gold for sprinkling (available here)

> pinch of salt

PREPARATION

Put all the ingredients (except for the erythritol gold) in a blender and mix it well until you get a homogeneous mass.

Fill your shake in a large glass and sprinkle it with erythritol gold as you like.

KETO CARROT CAKE WITH CREAM CHEESE FROSTING

INGREDIENT

- ➢ 1 pack of keto cake mix
- ➢ 250g grated carrot
- ➢ 2 teaspoons of cinnamon slices
- ➢ 120g cream cheese
- ➢ 20g powder erythritol
- ➢ Aloaf pan

PREPARATION

Preheat the oven to 175 ° C.

Finely grate the carrots.

Put the baking mixture with the cinnamon stick spice and the water in a
mixing bowl and stir until a homogeneous dough is formed.

Lift the grated carrots into the batter.

Pour the dough into a greased rectangular baking pan and bake it for about
50 minutes.

In a small bowl, beat the frosting ingredients together with a hand mixer.

Spread the frosting on the cooled box cake.

KETO CHEESECAKE WILD BERRY BARS

INGREDIENT

- ➢ 130 g butter
- ➢ 160 g almond flour
- ➢ 30 g erythritol
- ➢ 225 g cream cheese
- ➢ 1 egg yolk
- ➢ 40 g erythritol
- ➢ Some lemon zest
- ➢ 135 g sugar-free wild berry jam
- ➢ 50 g butter
- ➢ 30 grams of chopped pecans
- ➢ 60 g almond flour

> 15 g erythritol

> Asquare casserole dish (approx. 20 x 20 cm

PREPARATION

Preheat the oven to 175 ° C.

Line a baking sheet or baking dish with parchment paper.

Melt the butter and knead into a dough with almond flour and erythritol.

Pour the dough into the mold and press down lightly.

Pre-bake the base for 7 minutes - it shouldn't be firm, just start to brown slightly at the edges.

Then let the base cool down.

Mix the cream cheese, egg yolk, erythritol and lemon zest together.

Spread the cheesecake layer evenly over the base.

Spread the jam over the cheesecake layer.

Knead the butter, almond flour, pecans and erythritol into a crumbly mass.

Scatter the crumble over the jam layer.

Bake everything for 18-20 minutes, until the top is lightly browned.

Let the bars cool down completely before cutting.

KETOBOOSTER STRAWBERRY YOGURT BARS

INGREDIENT

- 100g sugar-free white chocolate drops
- 10g yogurt
- 45g fresh strawberries
- 30g MCT Creamer
- 150g sugar-free dark chocolate drops for coating
- An elongated silicone bar mold

PREPARATION

Melt white chocolate over a double boiler or in the microwave.

Remove the stalk from the strawberries, wash the strawberries and cut into small pieces.

Add the MCT Creamer and yoghurt to the melted chocolate and stir together.

Fold in the strawberry pieces and pour the mixture into small, oblong silicone molds.

Let the bars harden in the freezer.

Roughly chop the dark chocolate and melt over a water bath or in the microwave and cover the bar with it.

Keep the bars in the refrigerator.

KETO FRENCH TOAST WITHOUT BREAD

INGREDIENT

- ➢ 15 g melted butter
- ➢ 30 g whipped cream
- ➢ 1 egg
- ➢ 2 tbsp coconut flour
- ➢ 1/2 teaspoon baking powder
- ➢ 20 g erythritol
- ➢ 1 egg
- ➢ 15 g whipped cream
- ➢ 1/4 teaspoon cinnamon

> Butter for frying

> Powder erythritol for sprinkling

PREPARATION

Whisk all the ingredients together in a mixing bowl and pour it into a square, microwave-safe dish.

Microwave the toast for 90 seconds, then let it cool down.

Cut the finished mass into square pieces of toast.

Whisk the ingredients together in a tall plate.

Now pull the toast slices through the breading.

Melt the butter in a pan and fry the toast slices in it for 2-3 minutes on each side.

Enjoy the keto French toast with powdered erythritol and fresh berries.

KETO CHOCOLATE MERINGUE CAKE

INGREDIENT

- 3 eggs
- 115 g erythritol
- 100 g butter
- 150 g ground almonds
- 40 g coconut flour
- 10 g bamboo flour
- 50 g sugar-free dark chocolate drops
- 1/2 teaspoon baking powder
- 5 g baking cocoa
- 3 egg whites

➢ 50 g powder erythritol

➢ 18 cm springform pan

PREPARATION

Preheat the oven to 175 ° C with a fan oven.

Melt the butter and the dark chocolate drops.

Now put all the ingredients in a mixing bowl and stir them until you have a homogeneous mass.

Fill the chocolate dough into a (greased) springform pan and prebake the cake for about 20 minutes.

In the meantime, beat the egg whites very stiffly, this can take 10 minutes.

Add the powdered erythritol and the baking cocoa in portions and continue beating the mixture.

Take the cake out of the oven and spread the chocolate meringue on it and smooth everything over.

Bake the cake again for another 15 minutes, until the meringue is lightly browned.

Then let the cake cool and enjoy.

KETO CHOCOLATE SALAMI

INGREDIENT

- ➢ 350 g sugar-free dark chocolate drops
- ➢ 60 g sugar-free white chocolate drops
- ➢ 100 g butter
- ➢ 40 g pistachios
- ➢ 50 g hazelnuts
- ➢ 80 g almonds
- ➢ Powder erythritol for dusting

PREPARATION

Melt the butter and chocolate drops over a double boiler or gently in the microwave.

Chop the white chocolate into smaller pieces.

Lift the nuts and chocolate chips into the melted chocolate and butter mixture.

Let the chocolate and nut mixture cool in the refrigerator for about 30 minutes.

Then put the mixture on a large piece of cling film and shape it into a sausage approx. 5 cm thick.

Twist the ends and let the chocolate salami set in the refrigerator.

Dust the chocolate salami with powdered erythritol for the perfect look.

DARK KETO CHEESECAKE WITH CHOCOLATE ICING

INGREDIENT

- ➤ 50 g butter
- ➤ 15 g sugar-free baking cocoa
- ➤ 20 g gold flax flour
- ➤ 170 g almond flour

- ➢ 100 g erythritol
- ➢ 10 drops of natural vanilla flavor
- ➢ 2 eggs
- ➢ 300 g sugar-free dark chocolate drops
- ➢ 550 g quark (40% fat content)
- ➢ 225 g cream cheese
- ➢ 110 g erythritol
- ➢ 2 eggs
- ➢ 1.5 teaspoons of locust bean gum
- ➢ 80 g cream
- ➢ 150 g sugar-free whole milk chocolate drops
- ➢ Springform pan with a diameter of 14 cm

PREPARATION

Line the form with baking paper or grease it well with butter or coconut oil.

Preheat the oven to 175 ° C (175 ° F) fan oven.

Mix all the ingredients together and knead them into a dough until you get a homogeneous mass - make sure the butter is at room temperature, otherwise this step will take a little longer.

Press the base dough into your shape.

Carefully melt the chocolate drops.

Mix all of the ingredients together to form a creamy mass.

Then spread the cheesecake mixture on the bottom and smooth it out.

Now bake the cake for 50-60 minutes. For the last 10 minutes you can increase the temperature to 200 ° to brown the cake.

Tip: The cake should be a little browned and no longer wobble. If it has not yet gained a nice color and / or still seems a little unstable, bake it for another 10-15 minutes.

After the baking time, let it cool down completely before removing it from the mold.

Melt the chocolate drops with the cream in a saucepan over low heat and mix well.

Spread the chocolate icing on the cooled cake and let it harden overnight in the refrigerator.

If necessary, the cake can be decorated with baking cocoa, liquid chocolate or the like.

KETO SALMON-SPINACH LASAGNA

INGREDIENT

- ➤ 1 pack of lasagne sheets from Palmini
- ➤ 2 spring onions
- ➤ 1 clove of garlic
- ➤ 250 g salmon fillet
- ➤ 200 g cream
- ➤ 4 sun-dried tomatoes
- ➤ 150 g frozen spinach
- ➤ 100 g of grated cheese
- ➤ Salt pepper
- ➤ 1 tbsp olive oil

PREPARATION

Peel off the garlic and cut it into small pieces. Cut the spring onions into thin strips and the dried tomatoes into small pieces.

Heat some olive oil in a large pan and fry the garlic pieces and the spring onion strips in it.

Cut the salmon into small pieces and fry it as well. Add the spinach.

After frying it for a short time, remove everything with the cream and season the sauce with salt and pepper.

Rinse the lasagne sheets with water and line the bottom of an ovenproof dish with them.

Cover the bottom with a layer of salmon spinach and place another layer of lasagne sheets on top. Finish with a layer of salmon spinach.

Finally sprinkle the lasagna with cheese and bake in the oven at 175 ° C for 20-25 minutes until the cheese is golden brown.

KETO BAKED APPLE TART WITH ROASTED ALMONDS

INGREDIENT

- ➢ 1/2 pack Kuchenglück baking mix
- ➢ 130 ml of water
- ➢ 100 g sour cream
- ➢ 100 g whipped cream
- ➢ 1/2 sheets of gelatin
- ➢ 25 g powder erythritol
- ➢ 1/2 teaspoon gingerbread spice mix

- ➤ Some roasted almonds
- ➤ 2 - 3 tbsp apple-cinnamon fruit spread
- ➤ 1/4 apple (preferably Boskop)
- ➤ An 18 cm baking pan

PREPARATION

Pour the baking mixture into a bowl and mix it with water according to the instructions.

Pour the dough into a round, greased baking pan and bake the cake for 20-25 minutes at 175 ° C fan oven.

Let the cake cool completely.

Mix the powder erythritol with the sour cream and gingerbread spice mixture.

Soak the gelatin in cold water for 5 minutes and then dissolve it in the microwave with a small splash of water - make sure that it never boils!

Whip the whipped cream until stiff, now fold in the powder-erythritol-sour cream mixture.

Add some cream mixture to the gelatine and stir it together - this way there are no gelatine lumps and you prevent the gelatine from being too hot!

Now fold the dissolved gelatine into the cream and sour cream mixture.

Place a cake ring around the cake base and distribute the filling on it.

Place the cake in the refrigerator until the mixture is firm.

Spread the apple and cinnamon fruit spread on the cake and decorate it with chopped, roasted almonds and small apple wedges

KETO VANILLA ICE CREAM WITH HOT RASPBERRIES

INGREDIENT

- ➢ 300 ml whipped cream
- ➢ 30 ml MCT oil
- ➢ 1 egg yolk
- ➢ 30 g powder erythritol
- ➢ 1/2 teaspoon locust bean gum
- ➢ 5 drops of natural vanilla flavor
- ➢ For the hot raspberries
- ➢ 100 g raspberries (fresh or frozen)

> 20 g powder erythritol

PREPARATION

Put all the ingredients in a mixing bowl or stand mixer and mix everything until the mixture becomes frothy. You won't get the cream stiff because of the MCT oil, but that's not important in this case!
Pour all of the mixture into a shallow Tupperware box, put it in the freezer and let it freeze there for at least 6 hours.
Puree half of the raspberries and sift in the powdered erythritol.
Briefly boil everything together with the rest of the raspberries in a saucepan.
Place the raspberry sauce on a deep plate or in a bowl and place one or more scoops of vania ice cream on top.

KETO BROCCOLI SOUP

INGREDIENT

- ➢ 250 g broccoli
- ➢ 1 L vegetable stock
- ➢ 1 clove of garlic
- ➢ 2 tbsp olive oil
- ➢ 2 onions
- ➢ Salt, pepper
- ➢ 1 teaspoon creme fraiche
- ➢ Cheesepops

PREPARATION

Finely chop broccoli, garlic and onions and fry well in olive oil.

Pour in the vegetable stock and simmer over low heat for about 20 minutes.

Now mix everything with a hand blender and season to taste with salt and pepper.

To refine it, creme fraiche can be stirred in. The delicious cheesepops give the soup that extra crunch.

CLASSIC KETO CHICKEN SOUP WITH NOODLES

INGREDIENT

- ➤ 800 g soup chicken (filler)
- ➤ 1 pack of soup greens (leek, celeriac, carrot)
- ➤ 1 piece of ginger
- ➤ 1 onion
- ➤ 1 bay leaf

- ➤ 1 tbsp salt
- ➤ 1 tbsp peppercorns
- ➤ 2.5 liters of cold water
- ➤ Vegetables of your choice, e.g., carrots, cauliflower or broccoli
- ➤ 1/2 pack of Shileo noodles
- ➤ Fresh parsley

PREPARATION

Wash the chicken parts thoroughly or dab them with a paper towel.

Prepare soup greens: cut the leek into slices. Peel and roughly dice the celeriac and carrot.

Cut the ginger into slices.

Simply cut the onion in half with the skin on. The bowl gives the soup a nice yellow color.

Put the chicken parts and all the chopped vegetables in a large saucepan and cover with approx. 2.5 liters of cold water. Add salt, pepper and bay leaf.

Bring the contents of the pot to a boil and simmer for about 1 hour.

After the cooking time, take the chicken egg out of the pot and separate the meat from the bones.

Pour the rest of the soup through a sieve into another pot (the cooked vegetables are no longer needed).

Add Shileo noodles and, if you like, the filler (carrot halves, cauliflower & broccoli florets) to the soup and cook for 12 minutes.

Finally, add the meat and garnish with fresh parsley if you like.

WINTER KETO RICE PUDDING CAKE WITH PEAR & CARAMEL SAUCE

INGREDIENT

- ➢ 1/2 pack Kuchenglück baking mix
- ➢ 130 g of water
- ➢ 1/2 teaspoon gingerbread spice
- ➢ 150 g Shileo rice
- ➢ 250 ml coconut milk
- ➢ 500 ml of water
- ➢ 4 sheets of gelatin
- ➢ 10 drops of vanilla flavor
- ➢ 70 g erythritol
- ➢ 15 g butter
- ➢ 100 g erythritol gold
- ➢ 120 g sour cream

- ➢ 5 drops of vanilla flavor
- ➢ 50 g whipped cream
- ➢ 1 pear
- ➢ 1 pinch of gingerbread spice
- ➢ 20 g erythritol
- ➢ 18 cm springform pan
- ➢ Walnuts as a decoration

PREPARATION

Put the sour cream and the erythritol gold in a small saucepan and stir both together.

Let the mixture simmer for 50-60 minutes, stirring occasionally, on a medium setting, until it turns brown and has thickened nicely.

Add the vanilla flavored butter to the pan and bring it to the boil again.

Let the mixture cool down a bit and stir in the whipped cream so that you get a soft caramel filling.

Mix 1/2 pack of the Kuchenglück baking mix with water and gingerbread spices and bake in a greased springform pan (18 cm) for 25 minutes.

Then let cool down completely.

Place the bottom on a plate and put a cake ring around it.

Halve and core the pear and cut the pear into small pieces.

Put the pear pieces together with the erythritol and gingerbread spice in a saucepan and bring to the boil.

Let the pear compote simmer for about 5 minutes, until it has thickened a little. Then let it cool down.

Pour 500 ml of water into the Shilo rice and bring to the boil.

Simmer in an open pot for 20 minutes, stirring occasionally.

Then rinse the rice briefly in a sieve under warm running water.

Put the rice back into the pot and simmer with coconut milk, erythritol and vanilla flavor for another 25 minutes without the lid. Stir occasionally.

Soak gelatine sheets in cold water for 5 minutes.

Take the softened gelatin out of the water and melt it in the microwave with a small splash of water - 10 seconds will probably be enough.

When the rice has the desired consistency, remove it from the heat and stir in the liquid gelatin.

Spread half of the rice mixture on the cake base.

Spread over the pear compote and then the remaining rice mixture.

Put everything in the fridge for at least 2 hours until the rice pudding is firm.

Decorate with walnuts, pear pieces and caramel sauce.

KETO MACARONS

INGREDIENT

- 130 g almond flour
- 75 g soft butter
- 30 ml coconut oil
- 40 g ground almonds
- 50 g erythritol
- 1 pinch of salt
- 1 egg
- 25 whole hazelnuts

PREPARATION

Mix all ingredients together until a homogeneous dough is formed.

Shape the dough into small balls and spread them on a baking sheet lined with baking paper.

Press a hazelnut in the middle of each ball.

Bake the nut macaroons at 170 ° C top / bottom heat for about 12 minutes.

KETO VANILLA BISCUIT CREAM

INGREDIENT

- ➢ 75 g vanilla croissants
- ➢ 125 g mascarpone
- ➢ 50 g whipped cream
- ➢ 5 drops of vanilla flavor
- ➢ or the pulp of a fresh vanilla pod
- ➢ 20 g powder erythritol

PREPARATION

Whip the cream until stiff.

Place the mascarpone in a mixing bowl and stir in the vanilla flavor and powdered erythritol.

Fold the whipped cream into the cream.

Crumbled the vanilla crescents.

Alternate the cream with the crumbled vanilla crescents.

Decorate the whole thing with cinnamon, ground vanilla or a whole croissant.

KETO LINZER STRIPS

INGREDIENT

- ➢ 100 g butter
- ➢ 100 g powder erythritol
- ➢ 150 g almond flour
- ➢ 50 g ground almonds
- ➢ 2 eggs
- ➢ 1/2 teaspoon baking powder
- ➢ 1 teaspoon psyllium husk powder
- ➢ 230 g sugar-free strawberry fruit spread

PREPARATION

Melt the butter and knead into a dough together with the remaining ingredients in a mixing bowl.

Sprinkle the work surface with a little almond flour and roll out half of the dough about 0.5 - 1 cm thick.

Place the dough on a baking sheet lined with parchment paper.

Prick the bottom with a fork and spread the strawberry fruit spread on top.

Roll out the remaining dough thinly and cut into 0.5 cm wide strips with a dough edge (preferably zigzag).

Place the strips of dough on the base as a grid.

Bake the Linz wafers for about 20 minutes at 175 ° C until they are golden brown.

Then let cool and cut into bite-sized pieces.

KETO VANILLA CROISSANT CAKE

INGREDIENT

- ➤ 1/2 pack Kuchenglück baking mix
- ➤ 50 g dark chocolate
- ➤ 130 ml of water
- ➤ 180 g butter
- ➤ 180 g cream cheese
- ➤ 15 drops of natural vanilla flavor
- ➤ 45 g powder erythritol
- ➤ 75 g crumbled vanilla crescents
- ➤ Vanilla crescents for decoration
- ➤ Round springform pan (18 cm)

PREPARATION

Carefully melt the dark chocolate in the microwave or on the stove.

Put the baking mixture in a mixing bowl and stir everything with water to form a homogeneous batter.

Then stir the batter with the melted chocolate.

Fill the dough into a round (greased) springform pan, bake it for 20-25 minutes at 175 ° C and then let it cool down completely.

Cut the cooled base in half horizontally, put one of them on a cake plate and put a cake ring around it.

Crumble the vanilla crescents with your hands.

Beat the softened butter with the mixer for at least 3 minutes.

Gradually add the powdered erythritol and keep stirring.

Finally add the remaining ingredients and stir everything together.

Now spread about 1/3 of the vanilla croissant filling on the bottom.

Place the second cake base on top.

Brush the outside and sides of the cake with buttercream and decorate with the rest of the vanilla crescents.

KETO BAUMKUCHEN TIPS

INGREDIENT

- ➢ 3 eggs
- ➢ 150 g butter
- ➢ 10 drops of vanilla flavor
- ➢ 150 g erythritol
- ➢ 200 g whipped cream
- ➢ 100 ml almond milk
- ➢ 60 g almond flour
- ➢ 1 tbsp guar gum
- ➢ 50 g ground almonds
- ➢ 1/2 packet of baking powder
- ➢ 100 g dark chocolate
- ➢ 50 g whole milk chocolate

PREPARATION

Separate the egg whites from the yolks and beat the egg whites until stiff.

Melt the butter and then whip it together with the vanilla flavor and erythritol until frothy.

Now stir in the egg yolks and whipped cream in portions.

Carefully mix the almond flour, ground almonds, baking powder and guar gum into the mixture.

Then fold in the egg whites. If the batter is too thick, add the almond milk.

Preheat the oven to 200 ° C top / bottom heat (or if possible with grill function).

Line an 8 by 8-inch baking dish with parchment paper.

Now spread the first layer - about 2 tablespoons - on the baking paper and bake it for about 5 minutes until it is slightly brown.

Repeat this process until all of the batter is used up.

Let the tree cake cool and cut it into triangles.

Melt the dark chocolate and dip the pieces of Baumkuchen in it.

Decorate the tree cake tops with whole milk chocolate as you like.

FLUFFY SWEDISH LOW-CARB CINNAMON ROLLS – KANELBULLAR

INGREDIENT

- ➢ 4 eggs
- ➢ 250 g quark (40% fat)
- ➢ 150 g powder erythritol
- ➢ 250 g - 350 g almond flour
- ➢ 20 g gold flax flour
- ➢ 50 g coconut flour
- ➢ 200 ml warm, unsweetened almond milk
- ➢ 1/2 packet of dry yeast
- ➢ 1 teaspoon sugar
- ➢ 140 g melted butter

- ➤ 130 g powder erythritol
- ➤ 100 g ground almonds
- ➤ 100 g chopped hazelnuts
- ➤ 2 teaspoons of cinnamon
- ➤ 130 - 150 g powder erythritol
- ➤ Juice of 1/2 lemon

PREPARATION

Dissolve the yeast in the warm almond milk and let it rest together with 1 teaspoon of sugar for about 10 minutes.

Mix the other ingredients in a large bowl and then knead with the yeast mixture to form a smooth dough and let rise again for 30 minutes.

Melt the butter.

Mix the melted butter with the remaining ingredients and stir to a homogeneous mass.

Roll out the dough into a rectangle on an abundantly floured (almond) work surface.

Spread the filling evenly on the dough.

Roll up the rectangle from the long side and cut into 8 evenly sized rolls approx. 5 cm wide.

Grease a baking pan with butter and arrange the individual dough rolls in the baking pan.

Cover everything with a cloth and let rise for another 20 minutes.

Preheat the oven to 175 ° C top / bottom heat and bake the cinnamon buns for 30 - 35 minutes until golden brown.

Mix the powdered erythritol and the lemon juice to a smooth glaze.

Take the cinnamon bun out of the oven, let it cool down briefly and brush with the lemon icing

KETO WAFFLE BISCUITS

INGREDIENT

- 100 g butter
- 100 g powder erythritol
- 150 g almond flour
- 50 g ground almonds
- 2 eggs
- 1/2 teaspoon baking powder
- 1 teaspoon psyllium husk powder
- 50 g sugar-free dark chocolate drops
- 1 tbsp baking cocoa
- 1 tbsp chopped hazelnuts
- Awaffle irons

PREPARATION

Knead together with the remaining ingredients in a mixing bowl to form a
dough.
Remove half of the dough and mix with the baking cocoa.
Shape the dough into balls about 2 cm in size and bake them in a waffle
iron.
Dip in melted chocolate if you like and sprinkle with hazelnuts.

KETO GINGERBREAD CREAM CAKE WITH CHOCOLATE GANACHE

INGREDIENT

- ➢ 25 g baking cocoa
- ➢ 450 ml water (50 ml more than what is written on the package)
- ➢ 600 ml whipped cream
- ➢ 40 g powder erythritol
- ➢ 8 sheets of gelatin
- ➢ 2 teaspoons of gingerbread spice
- ➢ 180 g of cream
- ➢ 150 g dark chocolate drops

PREPARATION

Mix the cake mix, baking cocoa and water in a bowl until a homogeneous mixture is formed.

Bake in a springform pan in the middle of the oven for about 40 minutes at 175 ° C.

Let the bottom cool down.

Soak gelatin sheets in cold water for 5 minutes.

Meanwhile, whip the whipped cream until stiff.

Sift powder erythritol and gingerbread spice into the cream and stir again.

Drain the gelatin sheets or squeeze them out with your hands and gently melt them in the microwave for 30 seconds.

Add some cream mixture to the gelatin and stir together - this way there are no gelatin lumps and you prevent the gelatin from being too hot!

Now add the gelatine mixture to the cream and stir in.

Place a cake ring around the cooled base and spread the gingerbread cream on top.

Put the cake in the refrigerator until the mixture is firm.

Bring half of the cream to a boil in a saucepan.

Add the hot cream to the chocolate drops and mix both well together. Then mix the second half of the cream (room temperature) with the mixture.

Then put the finished ganache on top of the gingerbread cream and distribute evenly.

Put the cake in the cold again.

KETO LEMON CAKE WITH WHITE CHOCOLATE

INGREDIENT

- ➢ 50 g almond flour
- ➢ 80 g coconut flour
- ➢ 250 ml almond milk
- ➢ 250 g quark
- ➢ 1 teaspoon Baking powder
- ➢ 1 pinch of salt
- ➢ 1 egg
- ➢ 2 egg whites
- ➢ 2 teaspoons lemon zest
- ➢ 1 pack FUNKY FAT FOODS - Vegan Organic WHITE
- ➢ 250 g cream cheese
- ➢ 2 teaspoons lemon zest
- ➢ 2 tbsp powder erythritol

PREPARATION

Preheat the oven to 180 ° top and bottom heat.

Mix all the ingredients for the base and put them in a greased pan.

Then bake the cake for about 25 minutes and let cool down completely.

Cut the cake in half horizontally.

Melt the white chocolate carefully in a double boiler.

Mix the ingredients together with the white chocolate until it becomes thick
and thick.

Spread the cream between the two halves of the cake.

Then spread them on the cake and coat the cake with them.

Put the cake in a cool place so that everything sets.

KETO GRANOLA BARS WITH RASPBERRIES

INGREDIENT

- ➢ 140 g Simply Keto Orient Crunchy Muesli
- ➢ 30 g nut butter
- ➢ 30 g coconut oil
- ➢ 10 g psyllium husks
- ➢ 50 ml unsweetened almond milk
- ➢ 70 g frozen raspberries

PREPARATION

Preheat the oven to 175 ° C with a fan oven.

Chop all ingredients (except for the raspberries) either in a stand mixer, a food processor or in a tall bowl with a hand blender - just briefly so that they are not chopped too finely.

Lift the frozen raspberries into the mass and distribute them in the silicone bar form (alternatively on a baking sheet lined with baking paper, approx. 1 cm thick).

Bake for 15 minutes until the surface turns golden.

Then let the mixture cool down a bit and cut it into about 10 long pieces.

Place the bars in the refrigerator or freezer so they can harden completely.

KETO CHOCOLATE MOUSSE TART

INGREDIENT

- ➤ 100 g almond flour
- ➤ 70 g butter
- ➤ 1 egg
- ➤ 50 g erythritol
- ➤ 25 g baking cocoa
- ➤ 240 g cream
- ➤ 150 g dark chocolate drops
- ➤ 180 g of cream
- ➤ 150 g dark chocolate drops

PREPARATION

Preheat the oven to 175 ° C with a fan oven.

Mix the ingredients for the batter in a bowl.

Use your hands to knead the dough into a firm mass.

Wrap the dough in cling film and put it in the refrigerator for about 10 minutes.

To do this, beat 120 g of cream with a hand mixer until frothy.

Bring the other half of the cream (120 g) to a simmer in a saucepan and remove from the plate as soon as it has boiled.

Chop the chocolate and pour the hot cream over the chocolate.

Stir until the two ingredients are well mixed.

Mix the frothy cream with the hot mixture - attention: just fold in slightly!

Take the dough out of the fridge and place it in a pre-greased baking pan (if you use a silicone baking pan, you don't have to grease it separately).

Bake the dough for 20-25 minutes at 175 ° C fan oven.

Let cool down well and then pour the chocolate mousse over it.

Put the tart with the mousse in the cold for about 10 minutes.

Bring the cream to a boil in a saucepan.

Pour the hot cream over the chocolate drops and mix both ingredients together well.

Spread everything on the tart.

Put the tart back in the cold for about 10 minutes.

KETO HALLOWEEN - BLOODY RED VELVET CAKE

INGREDIENT

- ➤ 4 eggs
- ➤ 250 g quark (40%) fat
- ➤ 120 g erythritol
- ➤ 150 g almond flour
- ➤ 20 g gold flax flour
- ➤ 30 g coconut flour
- ➤ 20 g bamboo flour
- ➤ 100 ml beetroot juice
- ➤ 100 ml unsweetened almond milk
- ➤ 1 teaspoon Baking powder

➢ 180 g butter

➢ 180 g cream cheese

➢ 15 drops of Simply Keto vanilla flavor

➢ 45 g powder erythritol

PREPARATION

Knead all of the ingredients in a food processor or hand mixer until you get a homogeneous dough.

Pour the dough into a round, greased baking pan and bake the cake for 30 - 35 minutes at 175 ° C fan oven.

Then let the cake cool completely.

Beat soft butter white with the mixer for at least 3 minutes.

Gradually add the powdered erythritol and continue stirring.

Finally add the remaining ingredients and stir in.

Cut the cake in half in half.

Place a layer of cake on a serving plate and brush with about 1/3 buttercream. Put on the second cake base.

Brush the outside of the cake with buttercream.

Sprinkle with sugar-free jam if you like and stick a small kitchen knife or scissors in the middle.

VEGAN & KETO NUT-COCONUT BARS

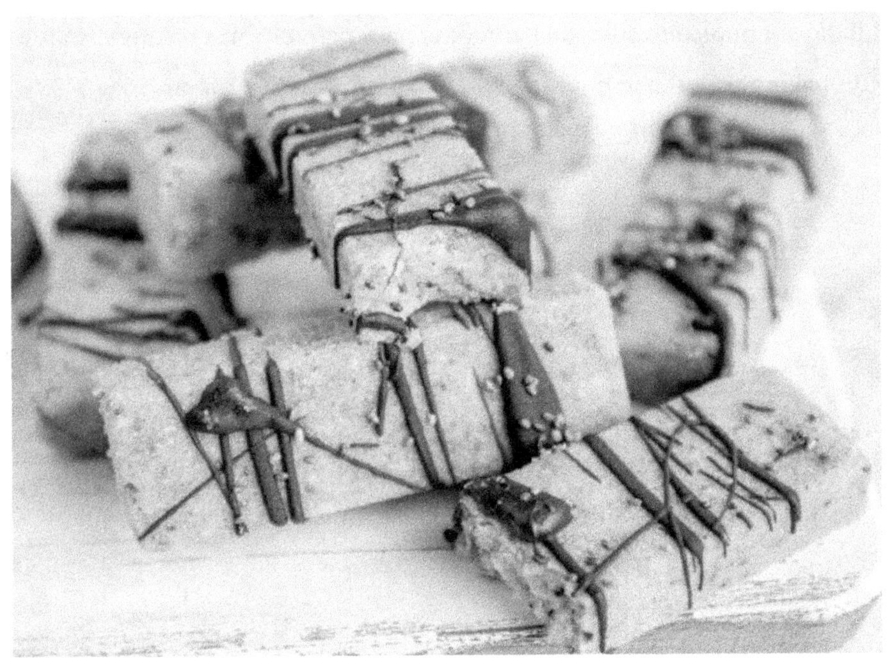

INGREDIENT

- ➢ 100 g almond butter
- ➢ 50 g coconut oil
- ➢ 200 ml unsweetened almond milk
- ➢ 60 g erythritol
- ➢ 40 g coconut flour
- ➢ 15 g chia seeds
- ➢ 15 g desiccated coconut
- ➢ 15 g of chopped almonds

PREPARATION

Melt the coconut oil carefully and stir together with the remaining ingredients in a mixing bowl to a homogeneous mass.

Fill the nut mass into silicone bar molds (alternatively on a baking dish lined with baking paper) and chill in the refrigerator for 1 to 2 hours.

Decorate the bars with melted chocolate as desired.

KETO POPPY SEED CAKE WITH CRUMBLE FROM THE TRAY

INGREDIENT

- ➢ 1 pack Kuchenglück baking mix
- ➢ 260 ml of water
- ➢ 5 drops of vanilla flavor
- ➢ 1 egg
- ➢ 100 ml whipped cream
- ➢ 35 g butter
- ➢ 25 g erythritol
- ➢ 100 g ground almonds
- ➢ 80 g erythritol

➢ 80 g butter

➢ 1 pinch of salt

PREPARATION

Mix the packet of Kuchenglück Baking Mix with water.

Place the dough in a square baking pan or on a baking tray lined with baking paper.

Boil the cream with butter, vanilla flavor and erythritol.

Stir in the poppy seeds and let the poppy seed mixture simmer for about 5 minutes until the poppy seeds are swollen.

Let the mixture cool for about 10 minutes, stirring occasionally, and fold in the egg.

Spread the poppy seed mixture evenly on the cake base and prebake it for 20 minutes at 175 ° C fan oven.

Meanwhile, melt the butter.

Now mix all the ingredients for the crumble and knead them well.

Spread the crumble mixture in the form of small pieces on the hot cake base.

Bake the cake with the sprinkles for another 15 minutes, until the sprinkles are golden brown.

KETO RICE PAN WITH PRAWN SKEWERS

INGREDIENT

- ➤ 140 g Shileo konja circle
- ➤ 1 yellow pepper
- ➤ 1 broccoli (approx. 500 g with stalk)
- ➤ 1 carrot
- ➤ 1 small red onion
- ➤ 1 tbsp clean vegetable broth + 150 ml water
- ➤ 200 g prawns
- ➤ Salt pepper
- ➤ 2 tbsp coconut oil for frying

PREPARATION

Pour the konja circle with approx. 2 liters of water, add a pinch of salt and simmer for 20 minutes over medium heat.

Then pour off the water and let the rice steep in a closed pot for 10 minutes.

Divide the broccoli into bite-sized florets.

Peel the onion and cut into fine cubes.

Peel the carrots and cut into small cubes.

Halve and core the paprika and also cut into cubes.

Heat coconut oil in a large pan and sauté the cut vegetables over medium heat until the broccoli is tender.

Deglaze the contents of the pan with the prepared vegetable stock and add Shileo rice and season to taste.

Finally, put the prawns on skewers and fry them in a pan.

Divide the rice pan on the plates, serve with the prawn skewers and enjoy.

KETO SEMOLINA BALLS

INGREDIENT

- ➢ 50 g dried konja circle from Shileo
- ➢ 40 g powder erythritol
- ➢ 300 ml unsweetened almond milk
- ➢ 20 g butter
- ➢ 2 tbsp desiccated coconut for rolling
- ➢ Sugar-free jam as desired

PREPARATION

Crush the konja circle in a high-performance mixer until a fine powder is formed.

Mix the almond milk, erythritol, butter, vanilla flavor and the rice powder in a saucepan.

Let everything boil briefly while stirring and take the pot straight from the stove.

Cool the finished semolina and let it set.

Then shape them into small balls and season in desiccated coconut.

Serve the low-carb semolina balls with sugar-free jam and enjoy.

KETO RASPBERRY BROWNIE TART

INGREDIENT

- 60 g butter
- 290 g of water
- 1 pack of Simply Keto Brownie Mix
- 4 gelatin sheets
- 30 g powder erythritol
- 300 ml whipped cream
- 60 g fresh raspberries

- ➢ 1 sheet of gelatin
- ➢ 100 g raspberries
- ➢ 10 g powder erythritol
- ➢ A22 cm springform pan

PREPARATION

Melt the butter.

Mix the baking mixture with water and melted butter until a smooth batter is formed.

Put the dough in a greased, round springform pan and bake at 175 ° C for 20-25 minutes.

Then let it cool down completely and remove the bottom from the mold.

Soak gelatin sheets in cold water for 5 minutes.

Puree the raspberries and strain them through a sieve if necessary.

Meanwhile, whip the whipped cream until stiff.

Sift the powder erythritol into the cream and stir again.

Fold in the pureed raspberries in portions.

Drain the gelatin sheets or squeeze them out with your hands and gently melt them in the microwave for 30 seconds.

Add some cream mixture to the gelatin and stir together - this way there are no gelatin lumps and you prevent the gelatin from being too hot!

Now add the gelatine mixture to the cream and stir in.

Place a cake ring around the cooled brownie base and spread the raspberry cream on top.

Put the cake in the refrigerator until the mixture is firm.

Puree the raspberries and stir in the powdered erythritol.

Soak the gelatine in cold water for 5 minutes, remove it and melt it in the microwave with a dash of water for 20 seconds.

Stir gelatin into the berries.

Spread the fruit sauce on the cake and place in the refrigerator again until it has set.

Before you remove the cake ring, cut along the inside of the edge with a knife so that nothing sticks.

SUGAR-FREE PINK LATTE

INGREDIENT

- > 250 ml unsweetened almond milk
- > 50 ml beetroot juice
- > 1 - 2 teaspoons powder erythritol
- > Pimp it Pink organic spice as you like

PREPARATION

Heat and froth the almond milk. Mix with the powder erythritol in a tall glass.

Pour beetroot juice into the hot milk.

Sprinkle with Pimp it Pink spice as desired.

KETO TART WITH ROQUEFORT, FIGS AND WALNUTS

INGREDIENT

- ➢ 100 g almond flour
- ➢ 50 g coconut flour
- ➢ 1 tsp psyllium husk flour
- ➢ 1/2 teaspoon salt
- ➢ 1 egg
- ➢ 70 ml of cold water
- ➢ 2 tbsp olive oil
- ➢ 200 g crème fraîche
- ➢ 3 eggs

➢ 100 g of Roquefort cheese

➢ 2 fresh figs

➢ 50 g walnuts

➢ 2 tablespoons of sugar-free "maple" syrup

➢ A rectangular tart pan approx. 35 cm long

PREPARATION

Put all the ingredients for the dough in a mixing bowl and knead until a homogeneous dough is formed.

Wrap it in cling film and chill for 10 minutes.

Then roll out the dough with a rolling pin to about 0.5 cm thick. Tip: If you put cling film on the dough, the rolling pin won't stick to it!

Place the rolled-out dough in a greased tart pan.

Mix the crème fraîche with the eggs, season with salt and pepper and spread the mixture on the dough.

Then prebake the dough with the filling at 180 ° C top and bottom heat for 10 minutes.

Slice the figs, cut the Roquefort cheese into pieces and roughly chop the walnuts.

Top the pre-baked tart with fig slices, Roquefort and walnuts.

Bake the tart for another 10 to 15 minutes.

Then let it cool down a bit, remove from the mold, cut into pieces, drizzle 2 tbsp.

KETO COVERED APPLE PIE

INGREDIENT

- ➢ 90 g ground almonds
- ➢ 35 g almond flour
- ➢ 50 g butter
- ➢ 40 g cream cheese
- ➢ 1 egg
- ➢ 30 g erythritol
- ➢ 1/4 teaspoon locust bean gum
- ➢ 250 g apples

- ➢ 1/4 teaspoon cinnamon
- ➢ 30 g erythritol
- ➢ For the glaze
- ➢ 25 g powder erythritol
- ➢ 3 teaspoons of lemon juice

PREPARATION

Peel, core, and cut the apples into small pieces.

Put the apple pieces with erythritol and cinnamon in a small saucepan and let them simmer for about 10 minutes.

Knead all of the ingredients in a food processor or hand mixer until you get a homogeneous dough.

Put it in the refrigerator for 15 minutes.

Divide the dough in two and roll the dough out thinly between 2 layers of cling film.

Press one part into a round, greased baking pan so that the bottom and sides are covered.

Pour the apple filling into the cake pan.

Place the remaining batter on top of the cake and press the ends into place.

Bake the cake for 30 minutes at 175 ° C fan oven.

Sieve the powdered erythritol so that there are no lumps and stir it with the lemon juice.

Spread the icing over the cooled cake

KETO LEMON MERINGUE TART

INGREDIENT

- 180 g almond flour
- 10 g bamboo flour
- 1 egg (size M)
- 80 g erythritol
- 125 g butter (room temperature)
- 40 g erythritol
- 150 g quark
- 100 g yogurt
- Zest & juice 2 lemons
- 4 sheets of gelatin
- 3 egg whites
- 50 g powder erythritol
- Around 18 cm tart pan

PREPARATION

Preheat the oven to 175 ° C fan oven.

Mix all ingredients for the dough in a bowl.

Knead the dough into a firm mass with your hands.

Dust the dough sufficiently with bamboo flour and roll out.

Now press the dough into the greased form, prick it several times with a fork and bake for 12-15 minutes until it is lightly brown. Then let cool down completely.

Rub the lemon zest and squeeze the lemon juice.

Mix the quark, yoghurt, lemon juice, lemon zest and erythritol until smooth.

Soak gelatine in cold water for about 5 minutes. Then squeeze out and heat in the microwave until it becomes liquid.

Now stir the squeezed-out gelatine and the quark mixture.

Spread the lemon filling on the baked and cooled cake base.

Beat the egg white with the salt very stiff, this can take 10 minutes.

Add the powdered erythritol in portions and continue beating the mixture.

Spread the meringue over the lemon layer and smooth everything over.

Either flambé the meringue or lightly brown it in the oven for about 5 minutes using the grill function.

Then chill in the refrigerator so that the lemon layer solidifies.

KETO RED FRUIT JELLY WITH VANILLA SAUCE

INGREDIENT

- ➢ 250 ml whipped cream
- ➢ 1/2 teaspoon locust bean gum
- ➢ 1 teaspoon powder erythritol
- ➢ 5 drops of vanilla flavor

PREPARATION

Put the berry mixture in a small saucepan and heat.

Mix the erythritol and agar agar, this will distribute the agar better afterwards.

Now add the erythritol mixture to the berries and let everything simmer for 4 minutes - it is essential to keep to the time, otherwise the agar agar will not set later.

Pour red groats into preserving jars or bowls and allow to cool.

Heat the whipped cream, place in a tall mixing vessel and mix with the rest of the ingredients.

Let cool down briefly and pour over the red fruit jelly.